Your Sales

71 Tips

To SkyRocket Your Revenue

BY
Amelia Mimi Brown

Published by Soar2successPublishing
Visit our website at *Soar2SuccessPublishing.com*

ISBN: 9781943043484

Printed in the United States of America

Front Cover Photography by Alene Peterson Photography

TABLE of CONTENTS

DEDICATION

This book is dedicated to my Grandma, Nanny. At the age of 8, when she helped me with my first lemonade stand, she taught me one of the most important sales skills of all; you must be willing to get out and sell yourself.

No one can sell you better than **you**.

Even when you think they are buying a product or service, they are really buying **you**.

A NOTE FROM THE AUTHOR

If you're in business, you're in sales. Plain and simple. Most business owners have a passion for the business they are in or the product or service they offer. They may be passionate about the technical or creative side of what they do, but not the sales side. Being a rock star salesperson is what will keep you in business and, most importantly, will keep your business thriving.

This book is designed to give you the insights to skyrocket the profits. It will give you specific sales skills and sales system building tips.

Sales are the heart and soul of any business.

SALES MINDSET
TIP 1

CONVINCE YOURSELF FIRST

We are all given our own version of intuition. Some may "feel it in their gut," while others may "feel it in their bones." Everyone, including your potential clients, can sense the vibes you are putting out – whether you're doing it consciously, or unknowingly.

Your client can feel your passion and sincerity or your desperation and apathy. It shows up in your facial features, voice inflections, attentiveness, body language, and even in the way you walk in and approach them for the appointment. You are the first client that you must convince. If you don't believe in your product or service, your client will sense it and move on. List out all the reasons you were MADE to do this, WHY you are passionate about making sure others have access to it, and how others can benefit from it.

SALES MINDSET
TIP 2

KEEP 'EM SAYING YES

Your goal is to keep your client in constant agreement. It's easier to keep them saying YES versus moving them from a NO to YES. Find statements that you can make to keep them in a YES mindset. Tie-downs are a great way to do this. A tie-down creates an opportunity for quick and subtle agreement.

For example, you might say, "*Safety is one of the most important things to consider when purchasing a car, isn't it*?"

"Isn't it" is the tie-down. It would be hard for the client to say no. The magic question that will almost always foster a YES is, "*Is that fair enough?*"

Other tie-downs include: "*Wouldn't you agree?*" "*Does that make sense?*" "*Isn't that a nice feature?*"

"*Isn't that a great solution?*"

SALES MINDSET
TIP 3

EXPERT OR AMATEUR

Your potential clients only want to buy from winners; people who are experts. Would you want to be treated by a doctor who barely made it out of medical school? Chances are, probably not.

Ask yourself, *"Do I come across like an amateur?"* Amateurs rush into the sale. Amateurs don't prepare themselves. Amateurs come across as pushy, desperate, and impatient. Amateurs aren't seen to have the best interest of their client at heart.

Be an expert. Experts are well prepared. Experts appear cool and confident. Experts know their value and what they have to offer others. Experts always have the best interest of their clients at heart. Make sure your clients perceive you as a knowledgeable expert.

SALES MINDSET
TIP 4

YOUR INTERNAL DIALOGUE

What internal dialogue are you having with yourself around sales? Are you telling yourself that you can't make a certain amount of money? Or that sales is difficult?

Belief dictates behavior. What you "'think"' you are is what you will present to the world. If you find yourself with negative thoughts, put up affirmations that reinforce what you want to believe, how you want to behave, and how you want to present yourself to the world.

EX: *"I am a million-dollar salesperson." "I close all my deals." "I am AWESOME at sales."* Put these affirmations in places where you will see them daily. You will start to believe them. Your mindset will begin to shift, and you will begin to see new opportunities all around you!

BONUS: *AmpUpSuccess.com/SalesTipBook/SalesAffirmations*

SALES MINDSET
TIP 5

CREATE A SENSE OF URGENCY

You must create a sense of urgency for your client to take action. Most will put items and tasks in order of urgency.

If people do not have a sense of urgency about your service, chances are it won't be put on their list.

Think back to the last infomercial you saw. They use words like *"Limited Time Only"* and *"There's only space for 5 more people,"* Giving people a sense of urgency will trigger their sense of FOMO (Fear Of Missing Out). No one wants to miss out on something that could potentially ease a burden, solve a problem, or increase their income.

How can you create a sense of urgency?

SALES MINDSET
TIP 6

THE POWER OF THE PEER

People often look to the behavior of others for direction
and insight regarding the choices they make.
Looking to others for their recommendation is called social proof
or social influence. Make sure you are using this to your advantage.

Solicit testimonials from past satisfied clients and get their
permission to use these testimonials on your website, in
social media memes, and in your presentation material.
Ensure that you include the person's first and last name, title,
company name, and city/state. The more information that
is included about the person, the more likely someone is to
view the testimonial as credible. The more verifiable social
proof you have, the easier it will be for you to close the deal.

SALES MINDSET
TIP 7

FORECAST YOUR SUCCESS

Visualization is one of the most powerful tools you have in your arsenal. Your brain processes images faster than it can process words. If you see it, you can have it.

The next time you have a meeting or phone conversation scheduled with a potential client, take a moment beforehand to stop and visualize how you want that interaction to go. Have fun with it. Think: *"What's the best-case scenario or outcome of this interaction?"* Get in the moment and take yourself there mentally. Ask yourself, *"What does the room look like?", "What am I wearing?", "What things do I hear, feel, touch, taste, and smell?"* Bring in all your senses. Celebrate as if it's already happened. Get excited like your desired outcome is already yours. If you do this right, you won't be astonished when it happens, because you've already been there in your mind.

Bonus: *AmpUpSuccess.com/SalesTipBook/SalesVisionBoard*

SALES MINDSET
TIP 8

SET GOALS

Average salespeople don't set goals. They just wing it.
Exceptional salespeople set goals and give themselves an
incentive to help celebrate when those goals are achieved.
Make sure that you are setting S.M.A.R.T goals.
This means your goals are:

Specific
Measurable
Attainable
Relevant
Time-bound

If you are already familiar with S.M.A.R.T. goals, ask yourself,
"Have I applied this framework for all of my goals?" Remember,
just because you know something, it isn't enough.
Applying what you know and **taking action** is what matters.

SALES MINDSET
TIP 9

GET THEM INVOLVED

The quickest way to turn a potential client into a loyal client is to make it extremely easy for them to commit to buying something small-scale, so they can test it out before committing to a larger investment. This is like a trial run or a test drive. Make sure your trial offering is straightforward and in alignment with their needs.

Be sure you don't over-complicate things. Find easy ways to get them committed, like signing up for your weekly tips and eNewsletter, giving them complimentary access to an exclusive webinar, or downloading a free ebook, workbook, survey, or instructional guide from your website.

Each small-scale commitment should provide value and actionable steps that naturally and organically draw them into acknowledging their need for the full-scale products or services you offer, without being "salesy" or pushy.

SALES MINDSET
TIP 10

TAKE THE LEAD

Take the lead in conversations and discussions with your clients. Make recommendations, advise, serve, and assist your clients in a way that helps them realize the benefits and value you offer.

Taking the lead means you:

- Constantly look for ways to AMP Up Your Success (like reading this book!)
- Have your client's best interest at heart, are bold about serving and meeting their needs, and you're not afraid to be straightforward and truthful
- Ask the right questions from the start, directing your attention to them and what they need, not on you and what you do
- Focus on value and don't quote prices until you have built a relationship based on the KLaT Factor

SALES MINDSET
TIP 11

CHANGE YOUR WORDS

Your words matter. Words carry energy that creates emotions.
Use that to your advantage.
Strategically replace words in your vocabulary that will
positively influence the emotions of your prospect, and it will
make a difference in how they view you and your services.

Here are some examples of the Don't versus the Do:

DON'T / DO
Make an appointment / Create a visit
Make a suggestion / Make a Recommendation
Send a contract / Send an agreement or proposal
Ask them to buy or spend / Ask them to invest
Ask for the first payment / Ask for the initial investment

SALES MINDSET
TIP 12

BE REMARKABLE

Remarkable means worthy of being spoken or remarked about.

You want to capture the attention of busy potential clients. You do this by being memorable and ***remarkable***.

This includes the way you dress, how you speak, your marketing collateral, emails that you send out, how prepared you are for appointments, the knowledge you have, the service you provide, your follow-up protocol, the way you handle objections and concerns, the kind of briefcase you carry, and even the car you drive.

Answer this question: What kind of REMARKS do you want people to make about you when you meet people for the first time, make your presentation, and when you leave the room?

SALES MINDSET
TIP 13

SELLING IS SERVING

You are not a salesperson. You are a person who is serving and meeting the needs of others. When you put yourself in the position of serving your client, it's not about convincing them to buy something, it's helping them receive something that will be beneficial. Whether it's helping them transform and improve their life, solve a problem, close the gap between where they are and where they want to be, it's a service that you provide in a loving and passionate way. It will make their life or well-being better. Your product or service is the solution that fills a gap in their life, and you have provided that by serving them. Having a "Serving Mindset" shows them you care about them before, during, and after the sale has taken place.

SALES MINDSET
TIP 14

BE CONSISTENT

Jim Rohn said, "*Success is doing ordinary things extraordinarily well.*"

It is important to do the small things extraordinarily well on a consistent basis. Small things will add up to be big things. Big things will give you big results. Focus on doing one or two small things that you can learn to do well consistently.

For example:
- Making three vetted sales calls daily can yield huge results.
- Hand-writing 10 Thank You notes a week can rack up big referrals.
- Meeting 10 new potential clients a week can keep your sales funnel full.

IDENTIFY AND ATTRACT NEW CLIENTS
TIP 15

R.O.P.E. THEM IN AND WOW THEM

Research: Make a list of potential companies
or people you'd love to work with.
Observe: Check out companies on Facebook,
LinkedIn, in newspapers and on television.
Pay Attention: Keep up with who has won an award,
launched a new product, opened a new location,
or started a new division of the company.
Engage Them: Does something stand out that you've read
or observed? Send them a WOW card. A WOW card simply
congratulates them on their achievement. Write a personalized
note, attach the article, and provide your business card.

This is a great way to get on their radar and is
the first step to gaining a new client!

IDENTIFY AND ATTRACT NEW CLIENTS
TIP 16

FOCUS ON MMA

Focus on MMA every single day. MMA stands for Money Making Activities. These are activities that will bring money into your pocket, like sending out proposals, following up on leads, setting up discovery meeting calls, and making sales. Cleaning your desk or office, surfing Facebook, and organizing papers, are not MMA activities. If it is not an MMA activity, it should not take up your most productive work time.

Are you using your time productively? To be sure, do a time study and keep a record of what you do during your scheduled work time. Label each task with: Admin, Personal, Misc., and MMA. Keep track for at least one week.

More MMA=More Success!

IDENTIFY AND ATTRACT NEW CLIENTS
TIP 17

MOTIVATION BUCKETS

People buy for their reasons, not yours. It's important to identify and attract the right clients by tapping into their motivation for buying your product or service. Your job is to link into one of the following and convey how your product will:

Save time
Save money
Overcome a fear
Give them pleasure
Eliminate pain

Asking the right questions will help you arrive at what motivates them.

IDENTIFY AND ATTRACT NEW CLIENTS
TIP 18

SELL TO THE RIGHT PERSON

Kim Duke, Sales Coach, said,
"Never take a NO from someone who can't say YES."

Ensure that you have identified decision-makers and are crafting the right message to attract them to you, your product, and your service. Often, we are pitching to the people who are not able to make decisions. At the start of your discussion, simply ask for clarification on who can make decisions. For example, you might say, *"Is there anyone else who needs to be a part of the decision-making process?"* Asking this question early on will prevent you from spinning your wheels with the wrong person.

IDENTIFY AND ATTRACT NEW CLIENTS
TIP 19

TAP IN AND PROVIDE INCENTIVE

Are you tapping into your current happy
clients for more happy clients?

If you know that a client is happy with your products, ask her
for the names and contact info of other small business owners
who might also benefit from working with you. Referrals
are often an untapped or underutilized treasure trove of
potential clients. Tap into yours today. The next step would be
to provide an incentive. Once, I was in my favorite store and
noticed a sign, *"Try on our new jeans and get $10 off your next
purchase."* I ultimately purchased those jeans. How does this
relate to sales? Three things: They gave an incentive for getting
involved, they got me involved, and created an ownership
experience for me. How can you do this for your client?

RAKE IN THE REFERRALS
TIP 20

NEVER COLD CALL AGAIN

Referrals are the golden tickets to increasing your sales. Skyrocket your growth by engaging and leveraging your biggest assets — your clients.

Why cold call potential clients when you can utilize and leverage the connections of your already satisfied clients?

How do you get the referrals? Ask for them of course! People are four times more likely to buy when referred by a friend. Create a structure for how you ask for referrals. Build the system into your sales process as a follow-up step after you deliver the product or service.

RAKE IN THE REFERRALS
TIP 21

STOP ASKING FOR THE REFERRAL; ASK FOR THE INTRODUCTION

Make it easy on your client by cutting out the vague language. If you mention that you want a referral, they might assume that you are looking for names and numbers. Be clear and direct.

Ask for what you are really looking to receive; a warm introduction. An introduction is simply your client connecting you with someone that could use your help.

RAKE IN THE REFERRALS
TIP 22

GET YOUR TIMING RIGHT AND RAKE IN REFERRALS

Timing is one of the most important aspects of getting great referrals. Be on the lookout for the best opportunities to ask. Ask for the referral after your client has had a positive experience with your service. Did they just rave about their experience with you via email? Did they just tweet out how they just loved working with you? Those are the perfect instances to ask them to introduce you to your ideal client profile (See the next TIP #23). The most optimal time is right after you receive a glowing compliment.

Cash in on those compliments and follow up with something like: *"I'm thrilled to hear you are pleased with your experience working with me. Would you know of others, just like you, who could benefit from my services? Would you be willing to make an introduction? "*

RAKE IN THE REFERRALS
TIP 23

IDEAL CLIENT PROFILE

Create an ideal client profile. Be clear on WHO you serve. Outline a short description of your most desirable clients. What are their titles? Do you sell to HR professionals or VPs of Sales? What industries or companies do they work for? You'll want to target precisely your ideal prospect so you can clearly communicate that to your client and fully leverage the referral connections received. Stop putting the burden on the person you're making the request of to select people. Be specific on what your ideal intro looks like. To whom would you give the most value? Provide examples of the types of prospects that you're interested in connecting with. Tell them who your ideal/target client is. Include info such as: job title, industries, and types of companies they work for, as well as demographic details like age range and socioeconomic status.

RAKE IN THE REFERRALS
TIP 24

BE SPECIFIC

Make it easy on your clients by being specific with your request. Stay away from the generic, *"Do you know of anyone else who could use my services?"* That's too bland, an instant turnoff, and makes it extremely easy to say no.

Create a short description of the type of referral you want. For example, what are the titles of the folks to whom you would like to be introduced? It makes it easier for the client to brainstorm good fit prospects for you.

RAKE IN THE REFERRALS
TIP 25

USE THE "HELP ME" PHRASE

As you ask for the introduction, remember to frame the conversation as a request for their help. Why? People get great satisfaction from helping others. They especially love to help people they know, like and trust.

Start off by asking, "*I was wondering if I could get your help with something?*" By positioning it as an ask for help, you're setting yourself up for a worthwhile discussion while leaving the other person feeling good about helping you out.

RAKE IN THE REFERRALS
TIP 26

KNOW YOUR REFERRAL SCRIPT

Have you been at a networking event and realize you have no clue where to lead the conversation? Always have your 10 second referral commercial in your back pocket.

Here's an example: *"We've had much success helping solo entrepreneurs improve their marketing by providing a solid streamlined marketing plan."*

"Do you know of someone owns a small business and is looking to grow her business?"

Customize specific mini commercials for partners, clients and vendors to make it easy for them to refer you.

RAKE IN THE REFERRALS
TIP 27

MAKE YOURSELF REFERABLE

Ensure that the client understands the value that you bring to the service that you provide for people and their business. Position yourself as a resource and be willing to walk them through how you bring value to your clients in all stages of your relationship.

You might ask, *"What else would be helpful to know about the work I do to help you feel the most at ease with providing me with introductions?"*

RAKE IN THE REFERRALS
TIP 28

GIVE REFERRALS TO GET REFERRALS

Put the principle of reciprocity to work for you. Be the first to give a referral to your client. By giving quality introductions to them first, you will get quality introductions back. Be patient; it might not happen right away but you will stay top of mind when opportunities arise. Lay the groundwork for the referral by saying, "*Happy to provide a referral to you, I know you'd do the same for me.*" Whenever interacting with a client, pay attention to what they're telling you they need. It might be something personal like a plumber, or a dry cleaner. If you have a great fit in your personal network, connect the two. If you're in sales, more than likely you have an extensive network. Use those connections to bringing in some extra cash for your client. Go out of your way to refer business to them first.

RAKE IN THE REFERRALS
TIP 29

DEVELOP A REFERRAL TEMPLATE

Do all the heavy lifting for them. Create an already crafted introduction that they can easily forward on your behalf. Send it over and give them instructions on how they can customize it. The easier you make it on them to introduce you, the more likely and quickly they will get it done.

Aim for the strongest intro as possible. Make the process easy and smooth for your referrer by developing a template. A referral template is a script framework used to effectively introduce you. It takes the guesswork out for the person willing to provide an introduction.

AmpUpSuccess.com/SalesTipBook/ReferralTemplate

RAKE IN THE REFERRALS
TIP 30

WHAT'S YOUR REFERRAL INCENTIVE STRATEGY?

Creating a referral incentive encourages your clients to share the value you provided with other people. Turn them into loyal brand promoters. It's essential to get your clients on your side by offering something to them to help you out. It's all about the give to get concept. People are more likely to help you if they are receiving something of value in return. This will allow you to drive repeat referrals.

Four things to consider when creating your referral incentive strategy:

1. Create a catchy name for the program — a name that will entice people to want to know more.
2. Select rewards and benefits that your client will value.
3. Make the rules easy to understand and follow.
4. Develop simple sign-up methods and fast forward payout.

RAKE IN THE REFERRALS
TIP 31

FIND A POWER PARTNER

One of the best things you can do is to find a "partner-in-crime" or a power partner. Find someone who is in a complementary field who you can create a referral relationship with so you can share clients or refer business to each other.

This is an extremely inexpensive technique that will allow you to grow your client base.

RAKE IN THE REFERRALS
TIP 32

GET IN THEIR PHONES

Most people keep their cell phones tethered to their sides. Ensure that your contact info is easily accessible right in their cell phones. Post your email address, phone number and social media handles everywhere. Any correspondences that you send out should have your contact information easily displayed. This includes email signatures, invoices, postcards, business cards, and all social media channels. Ex: At a networking event, ask for their number, and send them a text so you can program each other's numbers into your cell phones.

Use the LinkedIn Find Nearby feature to connect with people instantly at the event by using your mobile device:

AmpUpSuccess.com/SalesTipBook/LinkedInFindNearby

RAKE IN THE REFERRALS
TIP 33

SHOW YOUR GRATITUDE

Start a Refer A Friend campaign as a way to say *"Thank You"* to your clients. A Refer A Friend program is a brilliant way to give back to your clients and show your appreciation for their support of your business. You are demonstrating that you care about them and appreciate their business. They are more likely to engage with your brand. When crafting the email sequence, use appreciation in the headline or description.

This simple use of language instantly demonstrates the purpose of the program.

RAKE IN THE REFERRALS
TIP 34

GO ABOVE AND BEYOND

Dazzle your clients. Exceed their expectations. Word of mouth is one of the most powerful tactics to proposal referrals. It doesn't come easy. If you want to get your clients excited about your service and refer it to their friend, you must impress them. Deliver them positive experiences. Often, it's the simple things that mean the most. Send them a handwritten thank you note. For coffee lovers, a $5.00 gift card to Starbucks would be ideal. You can delight them with unexpected but personalized experiences. They will be tripping over themselves to refer you! That would give you reason to smile! A smile will also dazzle your clients! A smile shows that you are approachable and warm. It's the easiest way to build rapport right away. It requires no training. Aim to smile to at least five people every day!

RAMP UP YOUR RAPPORT
TIP 35

LISTEN FIRST, SPEAK SECOND

Listening is a foundational sales skill. Your client
will reveal to you exactly what they desire and
how they want that need to be fulfilled.

"Listen" people into buying; don't "talk" yourself out of a sale.
By actively listening, you are demonstrating that you
really care. Lean into the conversation. Be more focused
on what you're hearing than in what you're saying.

Acknowledge what you've heard by saying, "*Hmmm*," or by using
non-verbal cues such as nodding your head and physically leaning
closer. Use clarifying statements to reiterate what you've heard.

RAMP UP YOUR RAPPORT
TIP 36

DO YOUR RESEARCH

Learn as much as you can about a potential client. Google their company and name. Use social media sites like LinkedIn or Facebook to do your homework.

The more you know about a person or company, the more prepared you will be during a conversation. This will also help you discover any common interests you may share — your alma mater, charities you support, or hobbies you have. Finding personal ways to connect to a business contact can help strengthen your credibility and connection.

Keep in mind not to reveal too much about what you have learned about them, unless they have specifically listed on their profiles – like LinkedIn. You don't want to appear too eager or even worse – look like a creeper!

RAMP UP YOUR RAPPORT
TIP 37

USE THEIR NAME IN CONVERSATIONS

Dale Carnegie once said, *"The sweetest sound to someone is the sound of their own name."* There is no truer statement.

Make it a regular practice to use your clients' name in conversation. Using their name personalizes the interaction and says to the client that "I recognize you as an individual and, in this moment, you have all of my attention and energy."

Remember not to overuse it because it will come across as insincere.

RAMP UP YOUR RAPPORT
TIP 38

STEP UP YOUR DRESS

When people first meet and interact with you, you want
them to view you as a successful peer. You want them
to think that success is oozing out of your pores.

Success breeds success. People want to work with people who
look successful. Your clothes should be neat, clean, pressed,
and fit well to your body and frame. Select timeless pieces that
accentuate your brand. If shopping is not your forte, consider
hiring a personal stylist who has an eye for design and can
match clothes and accessories that work well for you.

Stepping up your dress will make the right impression on
your clients and potential clients. Looking good on the
outside will make you feel spectacular on the inside, which
will then create a magnetism that draws people to you!

RAMP UP YOUR RAPPORT
TIP 39

GIVE GENUINE COMPLIMENTS

When done right, genuine compliments are an excellent way to build rapport with clients. They are remembered long after they are spoken. People like to be acknowledged and recognized for things they do, how they look, and how they make others feel.

The key is to make sure that the compliment is sincere. You will turn the person off if the compliments come across disingenuous. Make them specific. Don't just say, "*I like your office.*" Instead, focus on something specific within the office like artwork or furnishings.

Use LinkedIn to give another person or company a compliment by using the endorsement feature. Build your compliment muscle by making a commitment to give out at least one genuine compliment per day. It will surprise you how effective they are and how amazing you will feel in return.

RAMP UP YOUR RAPPORT
TIP 40

SEND THANK YOU NOTES

Building relationships is what sales is all about and gratitude goes a long way in building fruitful relationships. Handwritten Thank You notes may be viewed as "old school" by some, but because they are rare, they stand out as a unique and memorable experience – for both the giver and receiver.

An email may get looked over quickly and then discarded along with half the other emails flooding their Inbox. However, a handwritten note is held, read, and usually kept out in the open or pinned up on a board, keeping you top-of-mind. Not only that, but your handwritten Thank you notes also have a better chance of being talked about, which potentially leads to word-of-mouth referrals – the bread-and-butter of every growing business!

Set a goal to meet at least 10 new people each week, and then send them a Thank You note.

RAMP UP YOUR RAPPORT
TIP 41

THIRD-PARTY TESTIMONIAL STORIES

Show your clients how great your service is by recounting a past client's story, complete with astounding results. A third-party story demonstrates how your client's situation improved by working with you and how your service solved a similar problem. The key is similarity. You want your client to feel as if they share the same challenges with the person in your story, and that they too could experience the same awesome results. A good way to start off this kind of story is to say, *"I understand how you feel. My client, Kim, was in a similar situation as you and X product (or service) worked out great for her. So well, in fact, that she's sent me three other referrals!"*

Use on social media, too. It's an easy way to ramp up your rapport!

RAMP UP YOUR RAPPORT
TIP 42

K.L.A.T. FACTOR

What is your K.L.a.T. factor? People like to buy from
people that they **K**now, **L**ike, **a**nd **T**rust. How are you
at allowing your clients to get to know you?
Once they get to know you, do they like you? People interact
a lot more with people they like. Being likeable creates
and enhances opportunities for conversations at all levels,
and conversations are the heart of sales success.
Once they get to know you, do they trust you? Do they trust
the product, service, or information that you are providing to
them is honest, upfront, and within their best interests?
You will turn people off if they feel like you're being too
pushy or too "salesy." As sales guru Jeffrey Gitomer said,
"People don't like to be sold, but they love to buy."
I'd also like to add that they love to buy from
people they Know, Like, and Trust!

OVERCOME SELLING OBJECTIONS
TIP 43

A CONFUSED MIND SAYS NO

Never give your prospect more than three options when making an offer. Providing more options will only overwhelm them, and instead of taking the time to sort it all out, you'll just get a flat, "*No*." Narrow down your choices by only mentioning the options that are best suited for them. When people are overwhelmed, or confused by the choices presented, there's a high chance they won't choose any of them.

When it's time to present your options for the sale, make sure you've given them all the information about each choice, and then give them a next step that makes it easy to act. It also helps if you give them convenient, easy to understand choices in how to commit, sign-up, and pay.

OVERCOME SELLING OBJECTIONS
TIP 44

PRESENT THE GOOD AND THE BAD TO AVOID THE NO

It's imperative that you know your product or service inside and out, through and through. Do your homework. Your client will have more faith in you when you know what you're talking about, and it will create instant credibility and confidence.

It's an expectation that you are up to speed on every facet of your offering. Know what makes your product/service great, but most importantly, know what DOES NOT make it great. You want to be sure YOU bring up the downside first – this keeps you in the "lead" position, and able to direct the conversation.

Knowing the downside of your product will help you overcome objections early since you will already have an idea of what the person could say to oppose your offer. It won't catch you by surprise.

OVERCOME SELLING OBJECTIONS
TIP 45

THE PRICE

Don't bring up the price before you've had a chance to bring up the benefits. Once you've covered the details on how you or your product serve the client, make sure you are comfortable with getting the price out of your mouth. When it is time to mention the price, you want it to come across as matter-of-fact, like it's just a minor detail of the transaction. Don't assume that the price will be an objection. If they do happen to object to the price, keep asking deeper questions until you hit on the heart of the matter. Steer the conversation in a way that helps you truly understand what they need so you can create a match with your offerings. Their objection about price is rarely about the money – it usually comes down to value. Show them that it's a great value, and you've made your sale.

Be prepared for the discussion about price, but don't lead with or volunteer the information until the time is right.

OVERCOME SELLING OBJECTIONS
TIP 46

FIND THE OPPORTUNITY IN THE OBJECTION

After you have aired your dirty laundry, you must overcome that dirty laundry. To get prepped for this, try the following activity:

1. Get out a piece of paper and divide it into two columns. On one side, list every major objection that's potentially important to your prospect or that you've experienced and heard.
2. For every objection, write down a way to resolve that objection. Try to create up to five responses for each of them.
3. Turn them into the opportunities. Rinse and repeat. Practice them! Review your list before you meet with a client, so you are familiar. The more you practice, the better prepared you will be. The next time you receive an objection, it will be second nature to offer a thoughtful response.

AmpUpSuccess.com/SalesTipBook/Objections

OVERCOME SELLING OBJECTIONS
TIP 47

IT'S A NUMBERS GAME

The more people you get in front of you, the more people that can buy from you. On the flip side, the more people you get in front of you, the more people that can tell you NO. Hearing NO isn't necessarily a bad thing. In fact, you should expect it. You must get through a ton of NO's before you can get to a YES.

NO is something you must accept as a part of the sales process. Everyone is not going to want your product or service. Really, it's not meant for everyone, just your target peeps, and the folks that need what you have to offer.

Reframe the word NO. Turn that NO around and flip it, so you can move ON to your next YES!

OVERCOME SELLING OBJECTIONS
TIP 48

IT'S NOT NO TO YOU

When a potential client says no, they aren't saying NO to you. They are saying NO to the offer you made.

There is a difference.

Fear of rejection will often stop people from making the offering.

Don't turn it into a personal blow; it's just a professional, *"No."* They aren't turning *you* down.

OVERCOME SELLING OBJECTIONS
TIP 49

COUNT YOUR NO'S

Every single NO you receive gets you that much closer to a YES. Take inventory of the no's you receive before you get a yes. This will be your starting point in determining your YES-to-NO ratio. calculate your YES/NO average. Instead of no's being discouraging, it can become a game. Your confidence will start to build with each no you receive, since you will be aware of how close you are to a YES. The better you get at overcoming objections and presenting the value of your product or service, the fewer no's you will get before you get a yes, and you will begin to see your Yes-to-No ratio improve! Begin counting your no's and yes's today. Take charge of your results. If it takes you nine no's to get one yes, and you know you need to make three sales this week, then you have a clear goal of needing to reach out to 30 people, which equates to your 27 no's and three yes's.

OVERCOME SELLING OBJECTIONS
TIP 50

THERE ARE DIFFERENT TYPES OF NO

Learn the difference between a NO, and a noooo. The noooo is all about the difference in vocal inflection. A noooo might be a lot easier to overcome than a NO. The noooo might indicate that you haven't given them enough information to decide. The noooo has a lower tone with a question in their voice. A noooo seems to hesitate with uncertainty. It is much easier to overcome a noooo, because you can automatically sense that they need more information. When you get a straight *"NO!"* there is usually no turning back from that. The decision has already been made. Learn to recognize the difference between the two so you can better determine what your next steps are in the sales process. See more at:
AmpUpSuccess.com/SalesTipBook/TypesofNos

THE FINE ART OF FOLLOW UP
TIP 51

ASK THEM!

Ask for guidance from your prospect or client on the best way to follow up with them. If you are on a discovery call and there seems to be a fit for your services but not at that moment, ask them what's the best way to stay in touch. Then do it!

Add a reminder on your calendar or use your CRM (Customer Relationship Management) system to remind you.

Staying in touch with them through their preferred format of communication is all about adding value to your relationship. It shows you are thoughtful, consistent, and believe in what you are doing. When you add value to them before a sale is even made, it makes closing the deal even more possible in the future.

THE FINE ART OF FOLLOW UP

TIP 52

DEFINE THE NEXT STEP

As a part of your pre-follow-up process, it's imperative that you get your client to commit to the next connection point. This can make or break your ability to close the deal. The best time to get a commitment on the next meeting or conversation is at the end of the meeting or phone call you are currently in. Know your schedule ahead of time. Capitalize on that golden moment. Give them alternative options (see Tip # 60). Example: *"Let's follow up next week. Does Wednesday at 4 or Tuesday at 5 work better?"* Give the invite while you're still in front of them.

Once you've discussed your next connection point, be sure to send them an email within 24 hours to confirm your meeting or next call.

THE FINE ART OF FOLLOW UP
TIP 53

DON'T JUST CONNECT – ADD VALUE

Stop "checking in" or "touching base!" Get these words out of your vocabulary. Start connecting for a specific reason by providing value during every interaction. Your goal is to stay top-of-mind without appearing annoying or overbearing. You can add value by sending an article based on something you discussed in a previous meeting. Email it to them and don't mention anything about doing business with them.

Your goal is to provide something of value that keeps you on their mind. Set up a Google Alert on their company to be notified when something is happening in their business or in their industry that may affect them. There are many ways and reasons you can find to make a genuine connection.

THE FINE ART OF FOLLOW UP
TIP 54

FOLLOW YOUR CLIENTS ON SOCIAL MEDIA!

Keep tabs on your clients by following them on social media. LinkedIn, Facebook, and Instagram are excellent platforms to use. Share articles of theirs that you find interesting or relatable, comment on posts with something of value to add, and periodically like their status or updates. If you see that they've won an award or had a positive life event, congratulate them and share their posts.

You can even take it a step further and send them a handwritten note congratulating their efforts.

In your posts, shares, and notes, the key is to not mention selling or doing business together. Relationships aren't built on selling, it's all about genuine connection.

THE FINE ART OF FOLLOW UP
TIP 55

DON'T WAIT

Many salespeople let a hot lead cool off too quickly. They will have a hot lead and wait way too long to circle back with that person. Create a habit and the discipline of reaching out within 24 hours of receiving the lead.

Create a template email that makes follow-up easy. Scan your business cards into your CRM or send them off to a virtual assistant to do it for you. Set a reminder on your calendar to follow up with people. Add it as an appointment.

Make sure that follow-up is a regular daily practice. You must build it like a muscle. You want it to be like breathing and very natural.

THE FINE ART OF FOLLOW UP
TIP 56

BE SOCIAL INVITE THEM OUT

Do you have an upcoming event and could use a companion or a guest? Invite them to your next association or chamber of commerce event.

Are you an active volunteer for a local non-profit organization and they have an upcoming event such as a golf outing or wine tasting? Extend an invite to them requesting that they be your guest.

THE FINE ART OF FOLLOW UP
TIP 57

LET GOOGLE DO THE WORK

Set up a Google Alert for the name of the person or company that you are interested in working with. Google will send you an email every time that name is mentioned in the news or through a publication.

You can then send a quick note congratulating them on their achievement or mention that you saw their company in the news.

This gives you an excuse to reach out.

THE FINE ART OF FOLLOW UP
TIP 58

STAY IN TOUCH

Build in ways to "stay in touch" without seeming like a pest. Here are four ways to stay top of mind without being annoying:

1. Research the trends and changes in their industry. Send them an article that they might find helpful with a note that says, "*I saw this and thought it might be of interest to you.*"
2. Congratulate them on a recent achievement that you saw on social media.
3. Mail them a customized Send Out Card (Go to ***sendoutcards. com/mimibrown*** to check it out) with a fun message or photo included of the two of you.
4. Send a postcard through the mail with fun stamps; something that will grab their attention. When was the last time you received a "FUN" piece of mail?

THE FINE ART OF FOLLOW UP
TIP 59

CELEBRATE THEIR BIRTHDAY!

Being in the Facebook and LinkedIn era, we can
easily keep up with people's birthdays.

Everyone LOVES to receive acknowledgement on his/her
special day. Send your prospect or past clients a birthday
greeting either through a phone call, email, or text message.

If you want to really stand out, consider sending a
personally recorded video message. They will eat this
up and you will get major points for creativity and
originality. You will definitely be top of mind.

CLOSE THE DEAL
TIP 60

EITHER THIS OR THAT

When closing the sale, it's best to give your client the option of an alternative solution. If you only give them one option and they don't like that option, the conversation could come to a screeching halt. As Pat Benatar would say, *"Hit 'em with your best shot."* Give them two great options to choose from so they are presented with a choice.
Examples:
"Would you like your burger with fries or a garden salad?"
"Does Tuesday at 7pm or Wednesday at 8pm work better for you?"
"Do you prefer to place an order on your MasterCard or your Visa?"

When you give them an alternative solution that works best for you and them, they are more likely to agree to one of them – it's a win-win!

CLOSE THE DEAL
TIP 61

ASK FOR THE SALE

If you've done your job effectively and followed the sales process, the next logical step is to ask for the sale. Yet so many people in sales fail to ask because of fear of rejection.
Don't leave money on the table. Your client is EXPECTING you to serve them in a bigger way. That "service" is asking them to take the next step. Get out of your own way. Ask them to buy. If they say no, remember that they are rejecting the offer you made. They are not rejecting you personally. Effective closing takes time and practice. Take some time to write down various ways you can close the sale, and then rehearse them, out loud, in front of a mirror. This will help you be more confident when the moment comes!
For examples:
AmpUpSuccess.com/SalesTipBook/CloseTheSale

CLOSE THE DEAL
TIP 62

ASSUME THAT YOU'VE GOT IT

The assumptive close is one of the very best ways to transition into closing the deal. Assume that you've done such a great job at creating value for the client, overcoming their objections, and focusing on the benefits that they can't help but say *"YES"*! Having a positive expectation from the start can play out favorably for you in the end. By assuming that your product or service is a match for them, you demonstrate more enthusiasm, energy, and confidence.

These are definitely attractive qualities that will appeal to your client. It gives you an unparalleled leg up. This type of close is very low pressure. Be warned though, the assumptive close is only effective if you've done your job successfully and have demonstrated extreme value. If not done right, it can come across as pushy.

CLOSE THE DEAL
TIP 63

LET 'EM TRY BEFORE THEY BUY

Most people buy based on emotion and justify with logic. Create an environment and experience that allows the client to "own it" before they buy it. Establish the connection so they become emotionally attached to the product or service.

Examples: Car dealerships always get you to test drive the car, pet shop owners let you take the puppy or kitty home for a few days, clothing store clerks encourage you to try on that slim pair of jeans, and treadmill companies let you use the workout equipment for a no risk 30-day experience.

All of these examples create an "ownership" experience for the client. Subconsciously, the client doesn't want to part with something that they already own. How can you create this experience for your client?

CLOSE THE DEAL
TIP 64

GET 'EM INVOLVED

Getting your clients involved in the sales process is an effective way to close the deal. Engage your client by having them answer a question that assumes they are already involved in the sales process.

It propels them forward into the future and creates a sense of ownership. Your goal should be for them to have an owner's mentality, like the item is already owned.

Example: *"Would you like to complete the initial paperwork or would like for me to assist you?"*

CLOSE THE DEAL
TIP 65

BE LIKEABLE

If a client likes you, they will find a reason to buy from you. Flip that around. If they don't like you, they will find MANY reasons not to buy from you.

Building a relationship with clients is critical to your success, and it doesn't take a ton of time to do. Every good relationship starts with trust. Help the potential client to trust that you are being genuine, authentic, and real.

It's easy to establish trust. Just be yourself. You will appear more confident and self-assured. These are attractive traits to anyone who needs what you have to offer.

CLOSE THE DEAL
TIP 66

WALK YOUR TALK

Don't make exaggerated claims or over-promise and then not deliver. You always want your thoughts, words, and actions to be in harmony.

If you say that you're going to do something, DO IT. Each tiny word and interaction will add to your trust account or deplete from your trust account. If you promise to email them a document by the next day, DO IT. They are judging whether they want to work with you by your actions.

A small thing may seem insignificant, but it truly matters. Consistency is key. Your client is making the decision on whether they want to buy from you based on these micro interactions.

CLOSE THE DEAL
TIP 67

ORDER OF OPERATIONS

Always present the most expensive/premium option first, even in the case when you think that someone would NEVER buy that item. Next, present the middle of the road option, and finally the least expensive option.

By using this sequence, the client believes that the lower price option is a much better deal simply because of the way it was presented. People like options. They are driven by wanting to get a deal. The bonus for you is if there are options in the most expensive package that they'd like to obtain, they may inquire on how they can get those options without having to buy the top package.

This gives you an instant opportunity to negotiate because the client might have a serious case of F.O.M.O. (Fear Of Missing Out).

CLOSE THE DEAL

TIP 68

USE YOUR STREET CRED

Credibility is a powerful sales tool. It can be defined as integrity, but most importantly, it involves honesty and believability. In order to appear credible, three elements must line up: your words, your actions, and your ability to resolve objections before they come up.

Credibility also comes in another form. You can borrow credibility. You can use the credibility of the company and the advertising or marketing source to lend credibility to your product.

Was it reviewed in a highly respected trade journal? Are you advertising in the Washington Post? Were you featured on the news or a highly visible national TV show?

You can use all these elements to increase your credibility and the credibility of the item or service you are selling.

CLOSE THE DEAL
TIP 69

SATISFACTION CONVICTION

Go beyond the money-back guarantee. Create a satisfaction conviction. A satisfaction conviction means that you believe in your product or service so much that you are willing to lay out a large return in exchange for their satisfaction.

Showing your "satisfaction conviction" could come in the form of a promise that says you'll give them a 100 percent refund within 60 days of purchase, AND buy them a competitor's product, if they aren't satisfied.

People will rarely elect to use this option, yet it gives them a lot more confidence in you and your product.

They might think, *"Wow, they believe in their product so much that they are willing to give such a generous guarantee. I want to do business with them."*

69

CLOSE THE DEAL
TIP 70

GAUGE THE TEMPERATURE

Just like you might check the temperature of a swimming pool before diving in, you want to do a temperature check with your client before attempting your close. If they aren't "hot" or ready to buy, then it's not time to close them. Ask questions that give you clues as to how they're feeling about the offer, product, or service, so you can gauge whether they're hot, warm, or cold.

Examples:
"How does that sound so far?"
"How close is this to meeting your needs?"
"What do you think?"
"What additional values or benefits would you like to see added to this package?"
"In your opinion, will this do the job for you?"

CLOSE THE DEAL
TIP 71

FEEL FELT FOUND

Use the Feel Felt Found technique to overcome
objections and connect with your client.

Feel: I understand how you feel. I can understand
where you're coming from. This wording lets the
client know that you heard them and can relate.
Felt: Initially others felt the same way. You are acknowledging that
this initial thought is common and that the situation can change.
Found: What they found was that after doing X, Y happened.
X is what you want your client to do (purchase your service
or put a deposit down now). Y is something positive your
client will receive that he or she cares a great deal about.

ABOUT THE AUTHOR
AMELIA MIMI BROWN

Enthusiastic, Sassy, and an Energetic Fireball — that is
Amelia Mimi Brown.
Mimi, as she is affectionately known, helps individuals
and organizations AMP Up the volume in their lives,
leadership, and businesses. She mentors with passion,
guiding her clients to effectively strengthen and
elevate their leadership vision to new heights.
With over ten years of corporate training experience, a knack
for making meaningful connections with audiences, and an
insatiable appetite for helping others maximize their potential,
Mimi knows how to rock a platform, connect with a crowd, and
provide training so that others can effectively do the same.

Mimi's down-to-earth humor compels audiences to laugh
while they learn. She engages groups from the moment she
steps in front of them and leaves them with empowering tools
and focused mindsets they will use long after the lights
have gone out at the event.

Mimi is passionate about people, leadership and presentations. She is especially inspired to help people take their careers – and themselves – to unprecedented levels.

Mimi's honors include being recognized as one of Michigan's Oakland County Executive's Elite 40 Under 40, Ms. Michigan Plus America 2015 and a proud contestant on NBC's The Biggest Loser.

When not speaking, Mimi can be found hanging with her family, sweating it out in hot yoga and bribing her snobby kitty with treats in exchange for snuggles.

BE SOCIAL AND SHARE, LIKE AND FOLLOW MIMI ON SOCIAL MEDIA:

AmpUpSuccess.com

Facebook.com/HeyMimiBrown

Instagram.com/HeyMimiBrown

Twitter.com/HeyMimiBrown

Linkedin.com/in/MotivationalLeadershipSpeaker